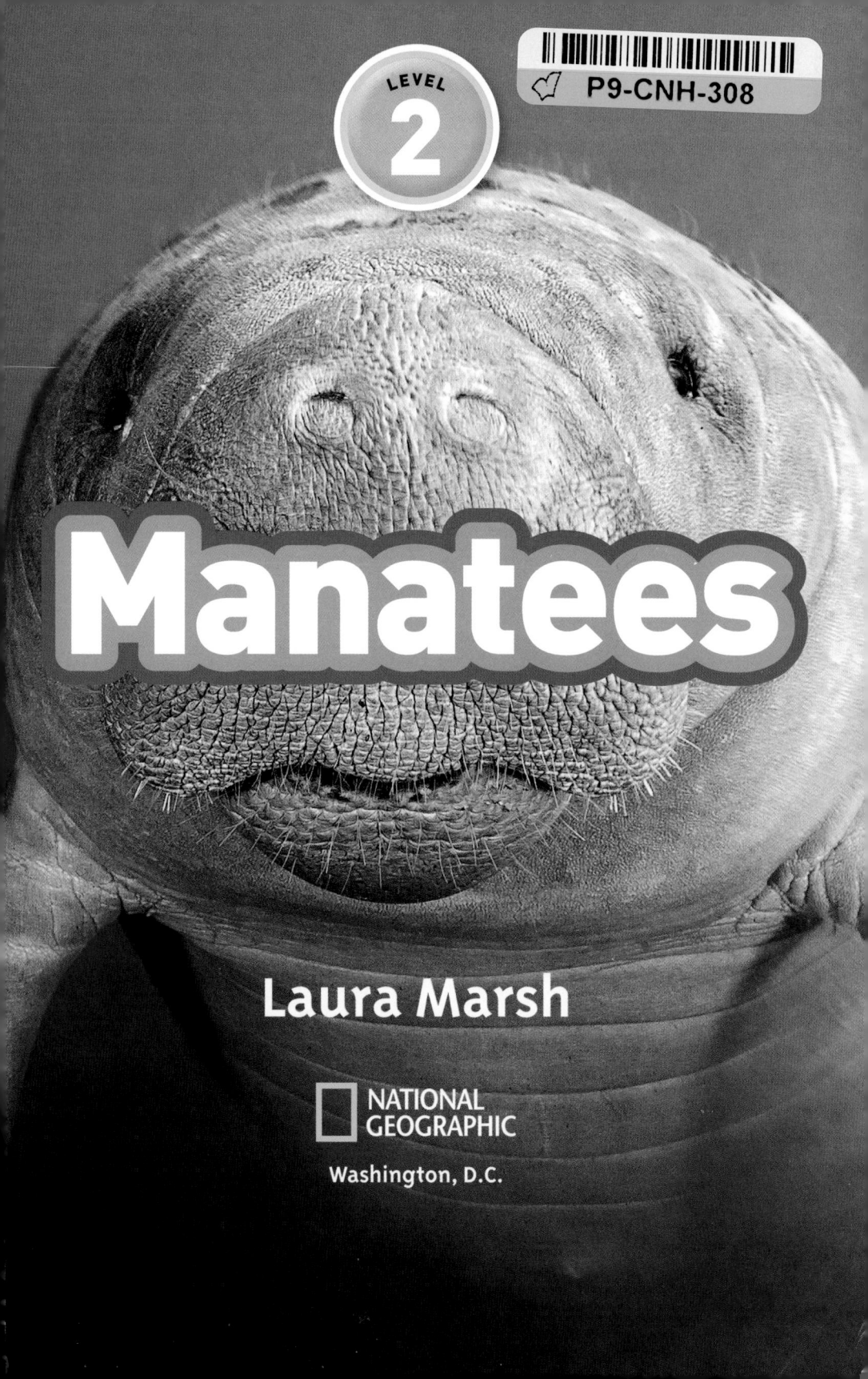

P9-CNH-308

LEVEL 2

Manatees

Laura Marsh

NATIONAL GEOGRAPHIC
Washington, D.C.

For Paul —L. F. M.

The publisher and author gratefully acknowledge the expert review of this book by Deborah Epperson, Ph.D.

Copyright © 2014 National Geographic Society
Published by National Geographic Partners, LLC, Washington, D.C. 20036. All rights reserved. Reproduction of the whole or any part of the contents without written permission from the publisher is prohibited.

Trade paperback ISBN: 978-1-4263-1472-8
Reinforced library binding ISBN: 978-1-4263-1473-5

Book design by YAY! Design

Cover, Brian J. Skerry/National Geographic Image Collection; 1, Masa Ushioda/SuperStock; 2, Luis Javier Sandoval/Oxford Scientific/Getty Images; 4-5, Alex Mustard/naturepl.com; 6, SuperStock; 8 (UP), Mike Kemp/Rubberball/Corbis; 8 (LO), Millard H. Sharp/Science Source; 9, Digital Vision/Getty Images; 10 (UP), Wayne Lynch/All Canada Photos/Corbis/Getty Images; 10 (LE), Visuals Unlimited/Getty Images; 10 (LO), Helmut Corneliimageb/SuperStock; 11, David Fleetham/Visuals Unlimited/Getty Images; 12-13, Dave Fleetham/Design Pics/Corbis/Getty Images; 14, Fred Bavendam/Minden Pictures; 15, Tom Brakefield/Purestock/SuperStock; 16 (UP LE), Jeff Foott/Discovery Channel Images/Getty Images; 16 (UP RT), Lonely Planet Images/Getty Images; 16 (LO), Mauricio Handler/National Geographic Image Collection; 16-17 (background), tristan tan/Shutterstock; 17 (UP LE), Jurgen Freund/naturepl.com; 17 (UP CTR), Pat Canova/Alamy; 17 (UP RT), Dorling Kindersley/Getty Images; 17 (LO LE), Franco Banfi/WaterFrame RM/Getty Images; 17 (LO RT), Wayne Lynch/All Canada Photos/Getty Images; 18, Richard Olsenius/National Geographic Image Collection; 19, Carol Grant/Moment RM/Getty Images; 20-21, Daniel J. Cox/Corbis/Getty Images; 22—23, Carl Mehler and Sven M. Dolling; 24, Will Vragovic/ZUMAPRESS/Newscom; 26, Biosphoto/SuperStock; 26 (inset), Jeff Foott/Discovery Channel Images/Getty Images; 27, Jurgen Freund/naturepl.com; 29, NHPA/SuperStock; 30 (UP), Greg Amptman/Shutterstock; 30 (CTR), Greg Amptman/Shutterstock; 30 (LO), Mauricio Handler/National Geographic Image Collection; 31 (UPLE), Greg Amptman/Shutterstock; 31 (UP RT), Dave Fleetham/Design Pics/Corbis/Getty Images; 31 (CTR), Wayne Johnson/Shutterstock; 31 (LO), Dave Fleetham/Design Pics/Corbis; 32 (UP LE), Alex Mustard/naturepl.com; 32 (UP RT), Fred Bavendam/Minden Pictures; 32 (CTR LE), Thorsten Milse/Robert Harding World Imagery/Getty Images; 32 (CTR RT), Paul Looyen/Shutterstock; 32 (LO RT), NHPA/SuperStock; Water Words header, Lonely/Shutterstock; vocab, Memo Angeles/Shutterstock

National Geographic supports K—12 educators with ELA Common Core Resources.
Visit natgeoed.org/commoncore for more information.

Printed in the United States of America
20/WOR/4

Table of Contents

Who Am I?. 4
Mighty Manatees 6
Super Swimmers. 10
Munching on Lunch. 14
7 Fun Facts About Manatees 16
Big Babies 18
On the Move 22
Manatees at Rest. 24
Keeping Manatees Safe 26
Stump Your Parents. 30
Glossary 32

Who Am I?

I have whiskers,
but I am not a cat.

I nibble on grass,
but I am not a cow.

I have gray, wrinkled
skin, but I am not an
elephant.

Who am I?
A manatee!

Manatees often rest in groups.

Q Where do manatees keep their money?

A In the riverbank!

Manatees are mammals that live in the water. They are sometimes called "sea cows."

Why?

Manatees are gentle and they move slowly, like cows. They also graze on sea grass, just like cows eat grass.

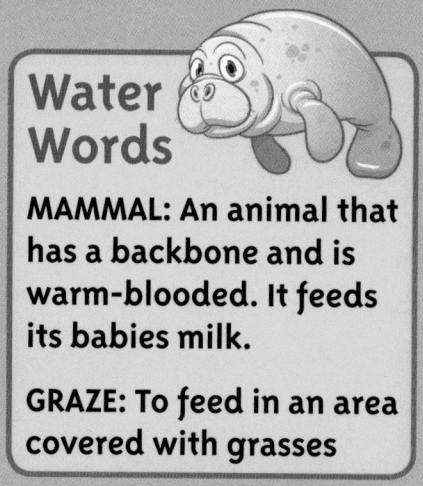

Manatees are big. They are usually about ten feet long. That's as long as two kids' bikes lined up end to end.

Manatees are heavy, too.
Most adult manatees weigh about 1,000 pounds. That's the weight of about 21 second graders!

Super Swimmers

Manatees can move their large bodies gracefully through the water. They swim upside down and roll. They even do somersaults (SUM-ur-sawlts)!

Q Why are manatees so wrinkled?

A Because they do not use irons!

A group of manatees swims in Crystal River, Florida, U.S.A.

Manatees don't like water that is too deep. They like to stay in shallow water in oceans and rivers. There, they find food and warm water.

A manatee's body is built for living in the water.

TAIL: It is large, flat, and round at the end. It moves up and down to power the manatee through the water.

EYES: They are small, but manatees can see well, even in cloudy water.
NOSTRILS: Manatees breathe air through these holes. But they close tightly underwater.
FLIPPERS: They help steer the manatee. They also bring food to its mouth.
LIPS: They are big and strong. They wrap around plants and pull them into the manatee's mouth.

Munching on Lunch

Manatees are herbivores (HUR-buh-vores). They eat plants for about six to eight hours every day.

A manatee grazes on sea plants.

Manatees have no front teeth. They don't need them because they don't eat meat.

Manatees have only large back teeth called molars. The molars help grind their food.

Water Word

HERBIVORE: An animal that eats only plants

7 Fun Facts About Manatees

1

They lose teeth all through their lives. New teeth replace them.

2

The elephant is a distant relative of the manatee.

3

Fat in the mother's milk helps a young manatee grow quickly.

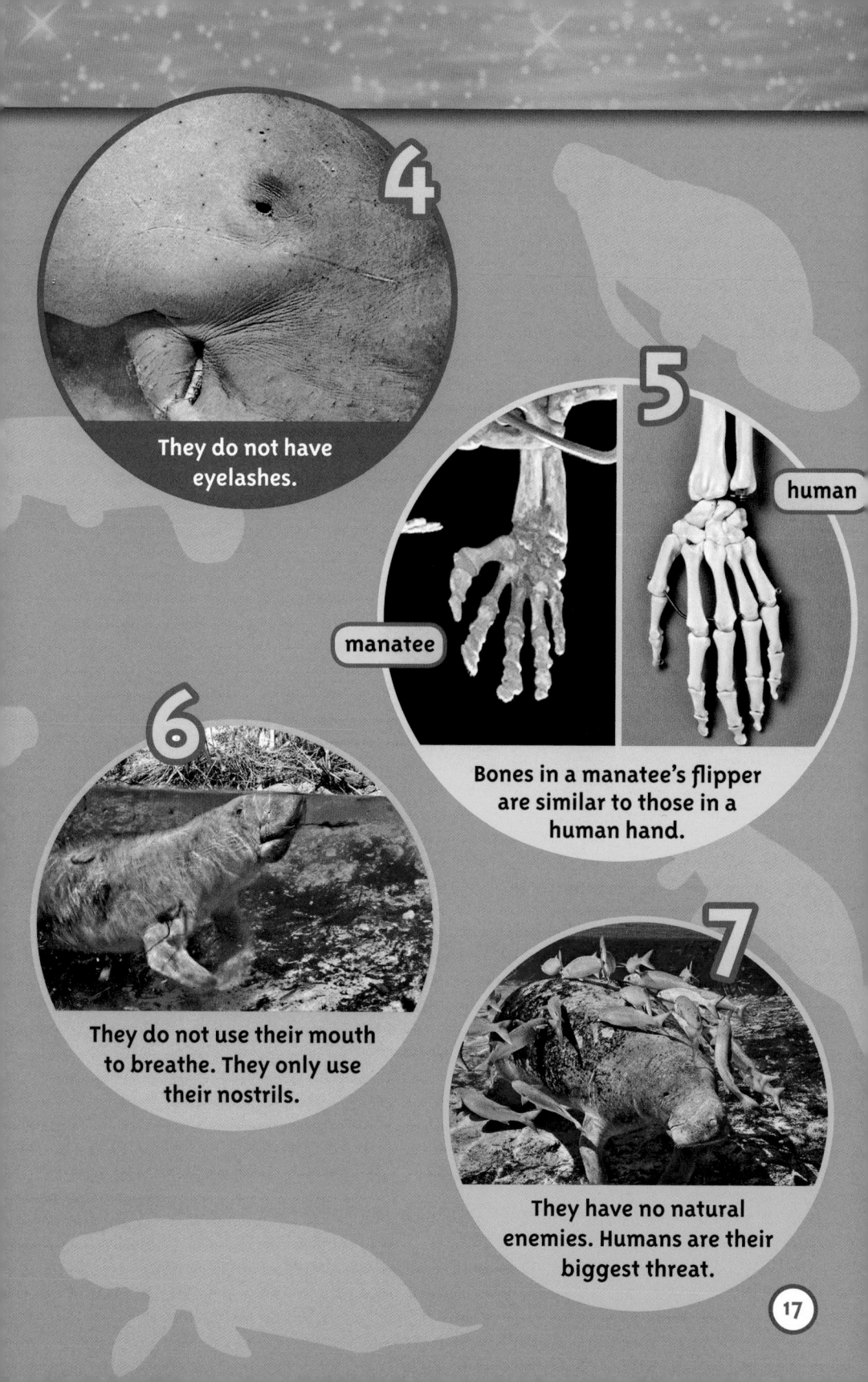
4
They do not have eyelashes.
5
manatee
human
Bones in a manatee's flipper are similar to those in a human hand.
6
They do not use their mouth to breathe. They only use their nostrils.
7
They have no natural enemies. Humans are their biggest threat.

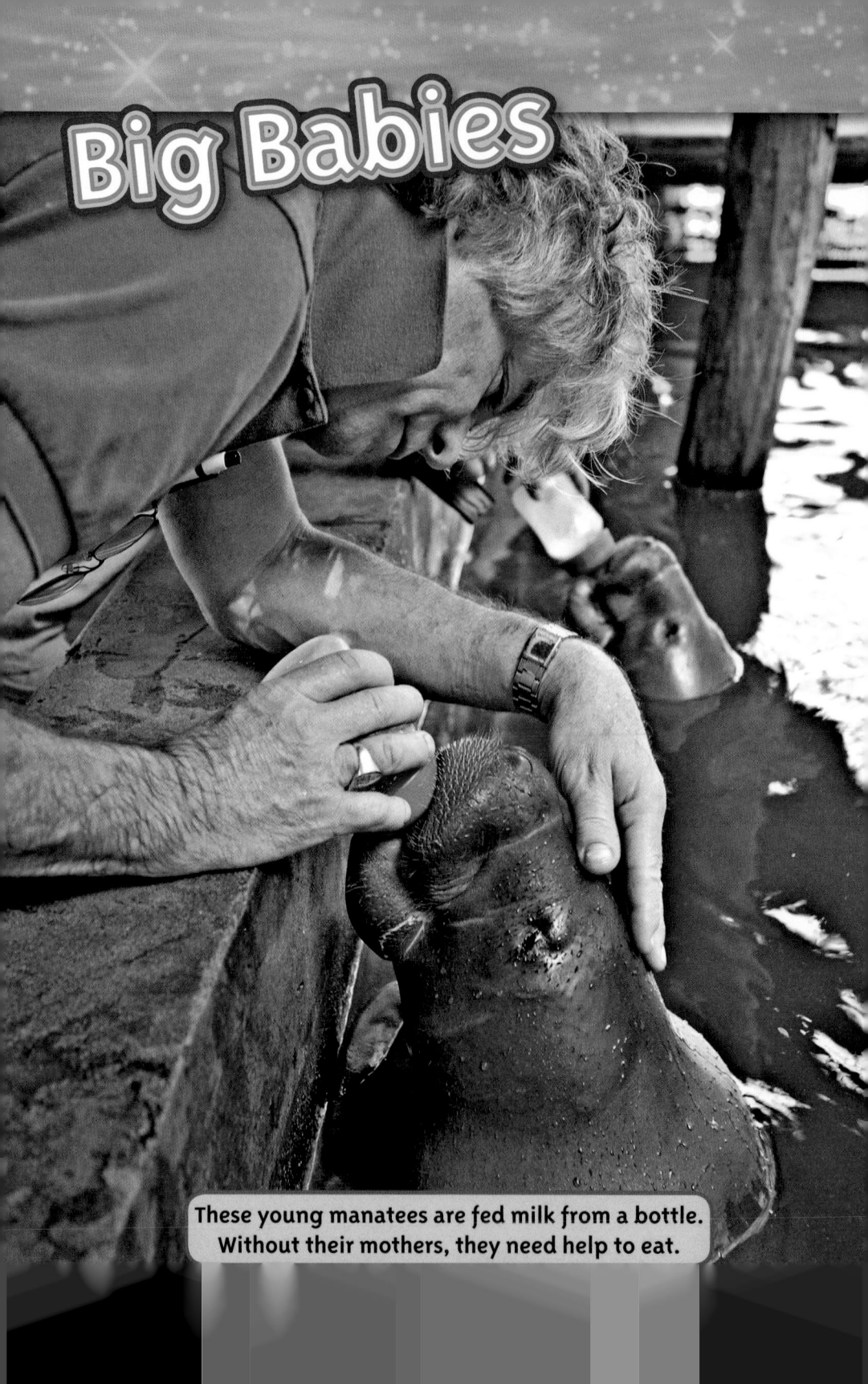

Big Babies

These young manatees are fed milk from a bottle. Without their mothers, they need help to eat.

A manatee baby is called a calf. It is born underwater. A newborn calf is about the size of a nine-year-old kid.

The mother pushes the calf to the surface to take its first breath. Within an hour, the calf can swim on its own.

Like other mammal babies, a manatee drinks its mother's milk. Soon it learns how to find sea grasses to eat.

A calf needs to stick with its mom.

Q What do manatees learn in school?

A Their A-B-Seas!

The calf must stay with its mother for the first two years. The mother teaches her calf how to live on its own.

On the Move

Manatees do not stay in one place. They migrate (MY-grate).

In summer, manatees can be found in many states. In winter, most manatees return to Florida. The water is warmer there.

Water Word

MIGRATE: To move from one area to another for food or a mate

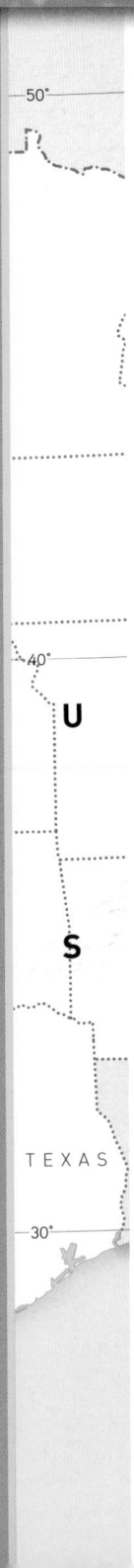

90°
80°
70°
CANADA
MILES
0
200
400
0
200
400
KILOMETERS
UNITED STATES
MARYLAND
VIRGINIA
Chesapeake Bay
NORTH CAROLINA
SOUTH CAROLINA
GEORGIA
ALABAMA
MISSISSIPPI
LOUISIANA
FLORIDA
ATLANTIC OCEAN
Area where Florida manatees live year-round
Area where Florida manatees travel in summer
GULF OF MEXICO
Florida Keys
Straits of Florida
BAHAMAS
23

Manatees at Rest

Manatees don't usually travel in groups. But they often rest together in warm water.

Manatees need rest, like you. But they don't sleep like you do.

They rest for about 15 minutes at a time. Then they need to come to the surface to breathe.

Manatees sometimes rest at the bottom of the sea or river. They can also float near the top of the water when resting.

Keeping Manatees Safe

There are many dangers for manatees. They are often hit by boats because they are big and slow and swim near the surface. Manatees can be hard to see in the water.

This manatee has scars from an injury by a boat propeller.

Q How do manatees turn their pancakes?

A They use their flippers!

People also throw trash and fishing line into the water. Swallowing trash can hurt manatees. Fishing line can get tangled around manatees so they can't swim.

Manatees are endangered (in-DANE-jurd). There are about 5,000 Florida manatees left.

But laws protect them. There are also special areas for manatees called sanctuaries (SANGK-choo-er-eez). In a sanctuary, people can't disturb manatees. They can live safely there and raise their young.

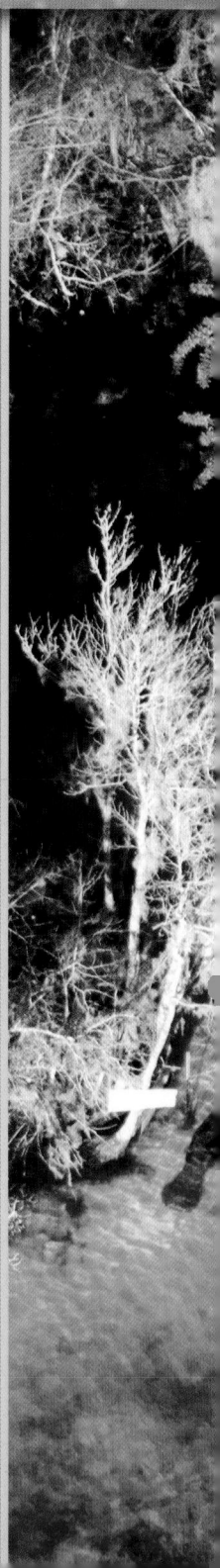

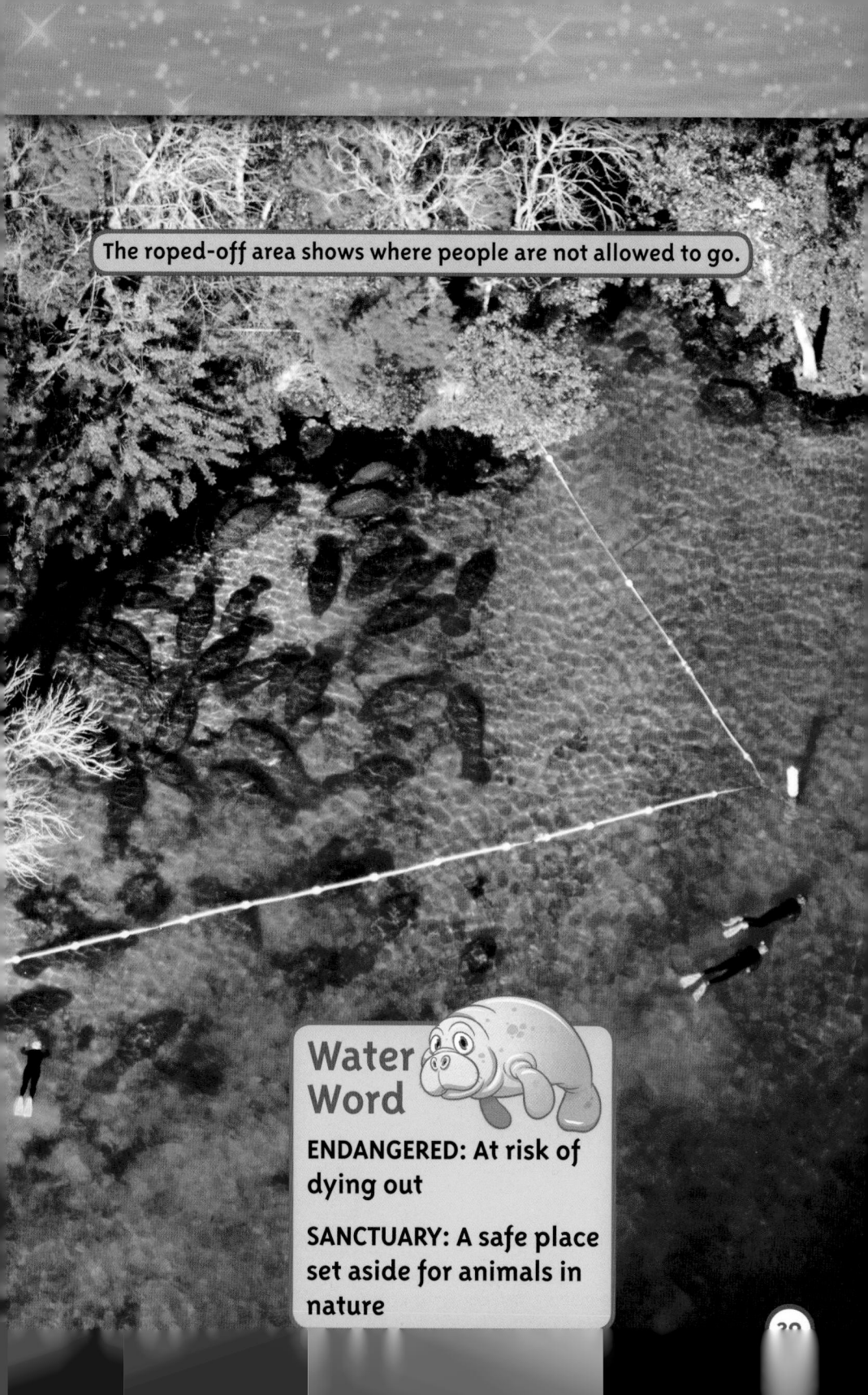

The roped-off area shows where people are not allowed to go.

Water Word

ENDANGERED: At risk of dying out

SANCTUARY: A safe place set aside for animals in nature

Stump Your Parents

Can your parents answer these questions about manatees? You might know more than they do!

Answers at bottom of page 31.

1

Where do manatees live?

A. In cool, refreshing water
B. In warm, shallow water
C. In deep, warm water
D. On the beach

2

A baby manatee is called . . .

A. A cub
B. A cow
C. A calf
D. A foal

3

What do manatees like to eat?

A. Plants
B. Crabs
C. Fruit
D. Steak

4

A manatee's lips . . .

A. Are very small
B. Are perfect for lipstick
C. Get in the way when eating
D. Grab and pull plants into its mouth

5

Manatees rest . . .

A. For many hours
B. For about 30 minutes at a time
C. For about 15 minutes at a time
D. Not at all

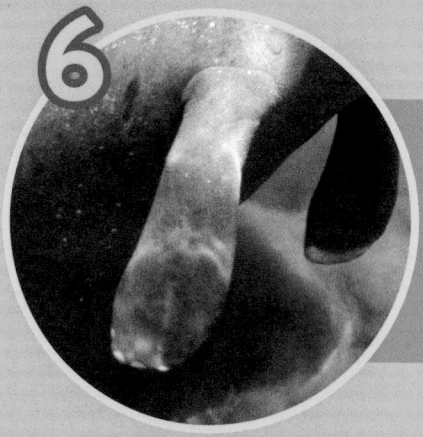

6

A manatee uses its flippers to . . .

A. Do the backstroke
B. Slap the water
C. Steer through the water
D. Wave to other manatees

7

To keep manatees safe, people should NOT . . .

A. Bother manatees in any way
B. Drive boats really fast
C. Throw trash in the water
D. Do any of the above

Answers: 1) B, 2) C, 3) A, 4) D, 5) C, 6) C, 7) D

ENDANGERED: At risk of dying out

GRAZE: To feed in an area covered with grasses

HERBIVORE: An animal that eats only plants

MAMMAL: An animal that has a backbone and is warm-blooded. It feeds its babies milk.

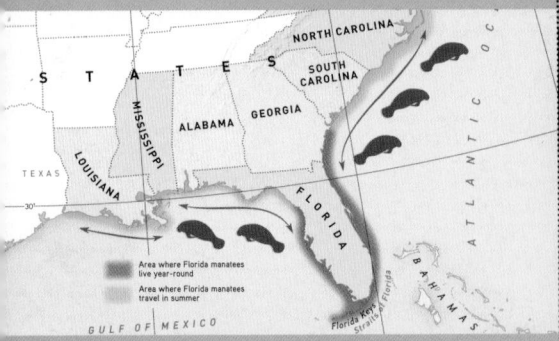

MIGRATE: To move from one area to another for food or a mate

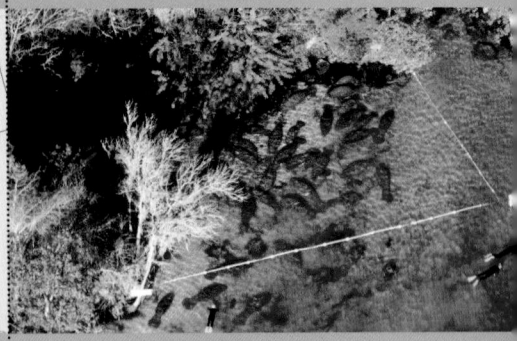

SANCTUARY: A safe place set aside for animals in nature